The Weekly Devotions for Salvation Series:

The Family Of Man

Comments by Bob Boyd

(52 Bible verses to support God's plan for man)

"But seek ye first the kingdom of God, and His righteousness;
And all these things shall be added unto you."

Order this book online at www.trafford.com/06-1987
or email orders@trafford.com

Most Trafford titles are also available at major online book retailers.

Note for Librarians: A cataloguing record for this book is available from Library
and Archives Canada at www.collectionscanada.ca/amicus/index-e.html

ISBN: 978-1-4251-0230-2

We at Trafford believe that it is the responsibility of us all, as both individuals and corporations, to make choices that are environmentally and socially sound. You, in turn, are supporting this responsible conduct each time you purchase a Trafford book, or make use of our publishing services. To find out how you are helping, please visit www.trafford.com/responsiblepublishing.html

Our mission is to efficiently provide the world's finest, most comprehensive book publishing service, enabling every author to experience success. To find out how to publish your book, your way, and have it available worldwide, visit us online at www.trafford.com/10510

www.trafford.com

North America & international
toll-free: 1 888 232 4444 (USA & Canada)
phone: 250 383 6864 • fax: 250 383 6804 • email: info@trafford.com

The United Kingdom & Europe
phone: +44 (0)1865 722 113 • local rate: 0845 230 9601
facsimile: +44 (0)1865 722 868 • email: info.uk@trafford.com

10 9 8 7 6 5 4 3 2

Dedication

I would like to dedicate this book to all my ancestors, who gave their life to Jesus, and prayed for the future generations to carry on the battle for the LORD! This book being an effort to simplify the questions that would remove all doubt that Jehovah is the only God and Jesus is the only way to get to Heaven. My heart-felt thanks go out to heaven for all of them.

A Big Thank You

I would especially like to thank my Mother who guided me spiritually throughout my life. Mom, I love you very much! It was you who gave me a Bible with a blessing (Hebrews 10: 21-39) in it when I graduated from high school in 1971. I still read that Bible daily. And this book is written because you took the time to teach me to be spiritual, not religious. Thank you!

I need to also thank my wife-to-be, Joanne, to whom I owe this springtime of my life. God gave us each other and I will be forever grateful unto Him that brought us together! I love you Joanne! Thank you so much for your love in return.

I also need to thank my good friend Pat Morrissey who has helped in editing this book. Pat has a command of the English language as well as possessing an outstanding amount of Historical knowledge.

Introduction

Where to begin is a challenge to a writer, as you my reader and friend, may remember from your school days. Genesis 1:1 opens with *"In the beginning God…"* which brings me to the point: God is the whole story of the world, and that includes you and all of us. It is God who made each of our lives for a purpose. It is my belief that God not only created the world, He had it all planned before He set His creation into existence. God spent only three pages on creation in your Bible, and the rest of the Bible was God divulging His plan for man.

In this series of books I use Bible verses along with commentary, points to ponder, and informal prayers. These prayers explore the characteristics of God, sometimes by a Hebrew designation, for those readers who may believe in God but as with so many souls in the world wondering, "Does God really care?" It is also for those of you who are familiar with the Bible to some extent but have not read it with the pre-planned creation as God's plan for man, a plan in which the family of man includes the *family* of parents and children made up of all men of all races and nations.

Even more amazingly, that the family of man is planned by God to include God The Father, God The Son, and The Holy Spirit (Holy Trinity) as a member. This greater family is to be the *Kingdom of God*, a *Holy Nation*, a kingdom or nation with a royal priesthood where love rules and selfishness in all forms is banished. Does this sound too good to be true? Without God's help it is!

Is God so loving to do all this for us? Well, 'yes'. This book explores the topics of love, wisdom and salvation among others.

This exploration is presented in 52 pages, to be read one-a-week either at home, in a study group or in structured religion classes. Each "Week" is numbered for easy reference, written in large print for your convenience using a simple format of a Bible verse from *The Living Bible*, then commentary in 'everyday' conversational language, with rhetorical questions to ponder and discuss with friends during the next week, and my personal impressions on some matters. I suggest to you to not only read the selected verse, but also read around it to get a "feel" for why it was put where it was and what was going on around that time. The "Week" ends with an informal prayer.

At the end of the 52 "Weeks" of this "year 1"it is my hope that you have a deeper appreciation for how carefully God plans, how deeply God loves us as mere mortals, how wise God is in guarding us when we are humble enough to know His will by prayer and study, and how unbelievable God blesses our obedience in both this life on Earth but even more so in Heaven!

The Family of Man lays out God's love inspired plan for man, using the Bible, the greatest love story ever written. The Bible tells us that God The Father sent Jesus Christ, His only Son, into our world to show us God's love, endure our human ignorance and evils, raise persons from the dead, show us Heaven and will by the Holy Spirit bring us into Heaven someday.

Thank you so much for entering into this adventure. May God bless you, your family and friends.

Table of Contents

Week One- Who is God?

Genesis 1:1 *In the beginning God created the heaven and the earth.*

When Moses wrote these God-inspired words, he was telling us that these were the most important words in the Bible. The first four words tell all. The whole plan starts with God, is about God, and is God. God is first and foremost in our minds.

We are told that there are three parts of God known as the Holy Trinity. There is God the Father, His son Jesus, and the Holy Spirit also known as the Holy Ghost. We will talk about Jesus later in this book. The Holy Spirit helps us to talk to God especially in those difficult times when it is so hard to pray. One part of the Trinity is just as important as the other.

God should be the first thought and last thought of each and every day. The whole Bible is about God, the "master potter". He made us out of dirt in His own image, the image of love. The Bible says on the sixth day He created man. I think He did more on that day. I think He created a plan of man.

There were things going on in heaven at that time. We get a glimpse of that in the first chapter of Job. Somewhere in that time God's "special" angel fell out of God's grace. This angel said he was equal to God. Do you think you are like Satan, the fallen angel, and equal to God? That angel was kicked out of heaven. He was relegated to rule God's footstool, the Earth.

I believe this is where the story of man begins. It almost seems as though God challenged Satan to see whom the creation would worship. Who are you worshipping?

A Prayer:

Father, I humbly ask for your favor to wash me clean of my sins and let me realize who You really are. As I begin this new venture, take me, break me, and make me a new creation in your image of love. Amen

Week Two

Revelation 22:13 *I am the A and the Z, the Beginning and the End, the First and the Last.*

This verse is from the last chapter in the last book of the Bible. In subsequent "Weeks" we will take verses from the Old as well as the New Testaments. God once again allows us to know that He is the Creator of all things. This verse has Jesus speaking as one part of The Trinity. The Trinity is God The Father, Jesus The Son, and The Holy Ghost. This verse was given to John from the 'resurrected' Jesus. This is where we begin to understand that God, Jesus, and the Holy Ghost had been there since the beginning of time.

At about the time, when 'time' was split in half (BC and AD), God sent His angel Gabriel to visit one of God's creations. Her name was Mary, and soon after that visit, she became pregnant with a child. Gabriel told Mary she would be blessed (impregnated) by the Holy Ghost and from that she would bear the Son of God. Gabriel told Mary to call her child Jesus. This is what we celebrate Christmas for.

There is so much to draw from this commentary. If He is first and last then He must be all there is. Who else in history has made this claim? What is most important is that God is the only God. He is the same as yesterday, today and tomorrow!

A Prayer

Thank You God for being my rock. I know I am in need of assistance, as You know how I messed up my life. I want You to take over my life and lead me where I am to go. My trust is in the One who created me. Amen

Week Three

Jeremiah 23:24 *Can anyone hide from me? Am I not everywhere in all of Heaven and Earth?*

God is a spirit who is omnipresent. He sees everything you do. This might not be good news for you, but it really should be. Are you thinking or doing something that you know God wouldn't approve? With God's eyes looking at me, well, can I say?

Webster's dictionary defines *omnipresent* as "present in all places at the same time". There is nothing that you have done that God has not seen. "Ouch"! I hear you. Perhaps it is time to remember that we all have sinned and come short of the glory of God (Romans 3:23).

The Bible tells us God is a spirit that has eyes that dart back and forth all over the Earth (2nd Chronicles 16:9). Just knowing this fact has made me change my attitude as well as my actions. It is my sincere hope that you will take this material to your heart.

Without getting ahead of myself, suffice it to say, that the plan for man that God created includes a way out of this sinful mess! This is not rocket science, just be careful what you do, because God is watching!

A Prayer

Father, help me to do your will, and then I will know that what You see me do is good in Your eyes. Thank you LORD for never giving up on me. My actions are now Your actions. Amen

Week Four

Job 42:2 *I know You can do everything and no thought can be witholden from You.*

Job was talking to God trying to explain that God knows every thought we think. He goes on to say: "You ask who it is who has so foolishly denied your providence. It is I. I was talking about things I knew nothing about and did not understand, things far too wonderful for me". Is this likewise true for us today? In Verse Five Job says he heard of God, but now sees God, and "loathes himself and repents in dust and ashes." Should we?

God knows what you want before you even ask Him. He is *omnipotent.* Webster's dictionary defines it this way "having unlimited power or authority; all-powerful". Who else do you know that was ever described this way? Have you gotten the idea now that maybe we should worship God with all our hearts?

This also means God knows what you are going to ask Him before you ask Him. So do not use repetitive prayers but pray from your heart to find His will in your matter. He wants us to talk to Him and listen to Him on a daily basis. If you aren't doing this, this would be a great day to start!

A Prayer

Father show me how to worship You with all my heart. You are like no other. You are to be praised above all. Amen

Week Five

2nd Samuel 22:31 *As for God, His way is perfect; The word of the LORD is true. He shields all who hide behind him.*

He is *omniscient.* Webster's dictionary defines it this way "knowing all things, the *omniscient* God". Wow, even the dictionary relates this word with God! Who or what else is perfect? Certainly neither I nor you are. Do you know anyone that is perfect other than God?

If God is everywhere at the same time, and is perfect in all ways, what else do we need to know? Should I end this book right here? Not so fast my friend. What does He want from us? How is He going to forgive our disobedience? Does He have an offer for us to choose eternal life? What do we owe Him?

I suppose we should move on to Week Six and see what we can learn about this wonderful God of ours. I encourage you to be meditating on these words and taking your time. In doing so you are building a very strong foundation. Remember: take your time because you are worth it!

A Prayer

Almighty and everlasting God, You are perfect in every way and I want to worship You and give You all the glory and honor You so richly deserve. Amen

Week Six

Isaiah 42:8 *I am the LORD! That is my name, and I will not give my glory to anyone else; I will not share my praise with carved idols.*

How could anyone get on their knees and pray to a carved statue? How can anyone pray to something that has died? I hope this book reaches the hands of those who think that way. All our praise goes to the One that is the same today, as he was the day before, and will be tomorrow. The LORD God Almighty, our living God, is to be praised.

In Verse 9, God continues on by saying everything He prophesied came true and He will continue to prophesy to tell us the future before it happens. Can you fathom how great that action by God is? Without God no mere mortal man could attempt such a feat. There are countless times man was told by God what to do, where to go, and what was going to happen and what was said happened. You ask how does God talk to man ?

I encourage you to ask Him to talk to you. For me, it usually happens at night in a "defining" dream. During the day I listen for that very still voice inside my head. This voice of intention convicts me as to the decision I am to make. Because of this, I do not believe in coincidences. I am driven by that little voice in my head, and it is for this reason why I have been accused of talking to myself by those who know me. If they only knew!

A Prayer

Father, I humbly ask for You to teach me how to hear You. Also, LORD, please teach me what You want from me. Teach me how to talk to You. Thank you. Amen

Week Seven

Deuteronomy 32:39 *Don't you see that I alone am God? I kill and make live. I wound and heal - no one delivers from my power.*

I believe God was explaining to Moses and Joshua to just "shut up and do what I say; I mean really, have I steered you wrong yet?" Read the whole of Chapter 32 and ponder this: How are you different than Moses? Why is it that man is so rebellious? Even today, we have many divisions in any one religion. For example, how can there be 32 sects of Presbyterians?

Do you think Jesus must be wondering what went wrong with His original concept? He said to love God with all your heart, soul, mind and strength, and to love one another as He loves us; and not all this other "stuff" of rules and regulations. (Mathew 22: 38-39) I believe that rules and regulations in the hands of unloving people emblazon "control" and is the answer to why there are so many divisions in God's Kingdom. Power comes from control, and we all know absolute power corrupts absolutely!

What God wants us to have is a personal relationship with our Creator. How simple is that? It is about relationships not rules. Come on Church, wake up and smell the coffee! It is time to rise and shine! By the time you finish this book you will understand how it is that I believe God did not create religion and their denominations, man did. Also, you may better know that neither animals nor plants has this faculty which we are said to be "Made in the image of God".

A Prayer

Father, thank you for opening my eyes to see the error of my way. How I long to look through the eyes of love. Thank you for taking me back. Amen

Week Eight- Promises of God

Exodus 19:6 *And you shall be a kingdom of priests to God, a holy nation.*

Can you feel it? God is talking to you! Congratulations for on being assumed into the ranks of priests. You are to become a priest in a *Holy Nation*. Can you believe it? Do you think God knows what He is doing? Absolutely!

Peter refers to us priests as a peculiar people in 1st Peter 2:9. What will your robe look like? Are you going to wear a crown? What are you going to preach on? I guess you have some thinking to do!

The *Holy Nation* that is mentioned in this quote refers to a holiness which is inside of us. It is our hearts and minds that determine our dress and message. You are to develop a mind-set of royalty, pure in thought controlled by an unconditional love towards your fellow man. Sometimes a smile can be the greatest message to be delivered.

You are one of a kind and very special in God's eyes. He formed you in your mother's womb! Quit beating yourself up and let go. You are a priest in the making!

Every good and perfect gift is from above, coming down from the Father of the highest heaven. He chose to give us birth through the word of truth that we might be a kind of firstfruits of all He created!

A Prayer

LORD you are my king. I humbly ask to serve You in Your holy nation. I am reporting for duty. What are my orders? Give me strength to do Your will. Amen

Week Nine

Isaiah 32:17 *Then judgment shall dwell in the wilderness, and righteousness remain in the fruitful field.*

Justice will eventually rule the land, and out of justice will come peace. Out of peace and the effect of peace will come quietness and assurances forever more. These are wonderful words from our gracious Father to His Holy Man Isaiah. He is all about "righteousness" which is the foundation for our priesthood in His *Holy Nation*. Be fair-minded with love in your heart, and you will never condemn in judgement again. Let God be the judge. If only I could get there!

This study-booklet was for my benefit as much as it is for you. In the morning when I picked up where I left off and reviewed that which I typed the previous day, I was amazed. It had to be the Holy Spirit using my hands, because I am not that smart.

My attempt was to write in a journalistic style, determining who God is, what does He want from us, how this should be done here in this lifetime as soon as possible, how we should change our hearts to reflect the love of our Heavenly Father, and to be awarded God's gift of eternal life. You have to have these facts to make that decision. I believe that all of you know deep down inside there is something "bigger" than us, and I believe it was put there by God. It is because God loves all of us, and it is hard to believe that some choose not to believe that fact. Enough said.

A Prayer

Most gracious heavenly Father, I know You are there. I remember a couple of times my conscience told me to do something, and sometimes I listened and sometimes I didn't. I also remember when I listened, what I thought, happened. So much for me taking credit anymore, it was You talking to me. Thank you O' Holy One. Amen

Week Ten

Mathew 5:6 *Happy are those who long to be just and good, for they shall be completely satisfied.*

The best words that were ever written were written in red. Does your Bible have Jesus' words in red? I find it helps me meditate better on Jesus' words. This is our first New Testament verse. I was just trying to trick you. Week Two was from Revelation and had Jesus talking to John. As you can see, all the books in the Bible make up "*one*" book. It lays out a beautifully designed plan by a creator for His creation. Many have tried to take a part of the Bible to justify a position when such a position is inconsistent with the rest of the Bible. Wrong, you cannot do that.

Our verse this Week is from The Sermon on the Mount, also known as The Beatitudes. Can you remember any other sermon by name? Is there anything you can't see from this verse? Do you want to be happy? Do you want to be completely satisfied? God told me to tell you over and over that you are worth it! Of course you are, again I say, you would have to be from another planet not to understand what God is saying to us that He really does love us!

We are beginning to put the first row of bricks on our foundation of our Holy Temple. We know who God is, and now in the next few weeks He is going to show us how to live our lives. Can you believe it has been two months already?

A Prayer

Almighty and everlasting Father, I long to be happy and satisfied. Please forgive me for trying to live my life by my efforts. I long to know real happiness and satisfaction. I now see, You promise it to me, if I will trust in You. Give me strength to battle those selfish thoughts in my head that keep me from You. Thank you LORD. Amen

Week Eleven

John 17:23 *I in them and You in me, all being perfected into one so that the world will know You sent me and will understand that You love them as much as You love me.*

This excerpt is a part of a prayer that Jesus was praying on Holy Thursday night right before He was going to be tried for treason and blasphemy. The whole of chapter 17 is that prayer. He was gathered with His disciples answering some of their questions. The end of that prayer also applies to each of us.

Jesus prayed, "O righteous Father, the world doesn't know You, but I do; and these disciples know You sent me. And I have revealed You to them, and will keep on revealing You so that the mighty love You have for me may be in them, and I in them." Think how much God loved Jesus, and then realize that God loves you just as much!

Jesus knew He was soon going to be put to death, yet He asked our Father to reveal the mighty love He has for us. Why did Jesus have to die? It just might be that God is speaking to you right now. Go ahead and listen, I'll wait for you. Remember to take your time! Did you realize there could be no resurrection without Jesus dying? Resurrection is what separates Christianity from all other religions!

A Prayer

O God, You are the God of Abraham, Isaac, and Jacob. It is Your power that I feel growing inside of me. Give me more I pray! I know You are the same God of yesterday, today, and tomorrow. Shower me with Your love. Praise you God. Amen

Week Twelve

Romans 11:16 *And since Abraham and the prophets are God's people, their children will be too. For if the roots of the tree are holy, the branches will be too.*

Paul was attempting to answer which was more important: Faith or Jewish rules? Paul's answer was faith which upset many Jews of his day. So when did God give Abraham His blessing? It was before he became a Jew! It was before he went through the Jewish initiation ceremony of circumcision. Abraham is the spiritual father of all of those who believe and are saved without being bound by the Laws of Moses. Abraham had found favor with God by faith alone, no laws having been revealed to him yet by God. This time period was way before Moses received the Ten Commandments from God.

Paul explains in Romans Chapter 2, verse 28, that a real Jew is anyone whose heart is right with God. Paul's point is that we are saved by faith in Christ, the fruit of faith being the good things we do. Faith backed by good works is what God wants. What a gift we have from our lovingly heavenly Father. It is called *Grace*, which is help from God for us to do good. *Grace* is free to those who believe that have a heart belonging to God! So long gentile tag, hello my Jewish friends!

I hope I didn't go too fast. I try to keep it simple. This was just another brick in our building a new life. I will build the case for Christ in a couple of months. We still have some more "first row" building to do. Now it is I who is taking my time!

A Prayer

Father, all I can think of is how wonderful your plan for man is, and I thank you from the bottom of my heart. Amen

Week Thirteen

2nd Corinthians 7:1 *Having such great promises as these, dear friends, let us turn away from everything wrong, whether of body or spirit, and purify ourselves, living in the wholesome fear of God, giving ourselves to Him alone.*

This statement sort of wraps up the first row. It is a review of the first twelve weeks. It comes back to "righteousness" and what it takes to be part of the *Holy Nation*. We are not to "fear" God for destruction, but to understand that someday we will have to account for our lives so we must always do good.

Again I say, this is not rocket science material. If you love someone, how can you do them wrong? If God has perfect love, then you know He will not and cannot do you any wrong. Do you want to run your life or let God do it? This decision is better made sooner than later. When the facts are presented about Jesus, maybe then you will understand what it means to love as God does.

I did not mean to come on so strong, but as I said earlier, this is the most important decision you will ever make. You must accept the fact that God wants to help you with your life. This is the beginning of wisdom. Wisdom, knowledge, understanding and discernment are the virtues we are seeking to enrich our lives! You are worth it!

A Prayer

LORD God, I humbly ask for forgiveness for not realizing how much You want to be helping me with my life. I ask for wisdom to hear you and see you throughout my day. I need You desperately, please come to me. Amen

Week Fourteen- Wisdom

James 3:17 *But the wisdom that comes from heaven is first of all pure and full of quiet gentleness. Then it is peace loving and courteous. It allows discussion and is willing to yield to others; it is full of mercy and good deeds. It is wholehearted and straightforward and sincere.*

If that doesn't say it all, what else could I say? It is possible to write a book on each of the above-mentioned guidelines. Since we all sin, in that we break these rules in our day-to-day living, we should take a hard look at ourselves and appreciate the *mercy* that God has shown us. He certainly could have destroyed the whole of mankind in the days of Noah. But, a master potter doesn't have to discard the vessel he is working on because of the defects in the clay, the master potter knows of ways to correct the mistake which an amateur wouldn't know.

God is our "master potter". He can fix things without starting over. His plan for man had numerous opportunities to change for the better, as He kept on top of it by performing different acts. The Exodus, the Flood, and a big one, which we will discuss in detail during the weeks coming up, are three examples of those kinds of "acts".

How are you doing with this information so far? As I said in the introduction to my book, I hope you have looked up in your Bible the verses I gave you; as well as reading around the verse to see what else that could be revealed. A concordance for references can help tremendously for additional information

A Prayer

LORD Hoseenu, our maker, to You all glory and honor. We owe everything to You. We praise your holy name. Thank you and we are eternally grateful to You. Amen

Week Fifteen

Isaiah 51:12 *I, even I, am He who comforts you and gives you all this joy. So what right have you to fear mere mortal men, who wither like the grass and disappear?*

I think God was showing Isaiah how insignificant man is as to God. The next verse has God saying to him, "You have no fear of God your maker; you have forgotten Him, the one who spread the stars throughout the skies and made the earth. Will you be in constant dread of men's oppression, and fear their anger all day long?"

That is not only what I wanted you to see, but also the words "He who comforts" which is a main point. This is another brick of wisdom in our building of a life. Have you figured out yet how much God loves you? Can you see His point of view towards man? How can we even think we can argue with God? Why would we want to? I have come to accept the only thing I fear is the idea of causing God, the eternal creator, any more pain. After what He did for me, I am sold hook, line, and sinker!

Friends, we are building wisdom. The teacher of wisdom is the Holy Spirit. He helps us to understand and discern God's plan for our lives. He will also go to God on our behalf, but more on that next week.

A Prayer

Jehovah Elohim, the eternal creator, build my character to the point of no fear of man. I want to satisfy You in every way. Amen

Week Sixteen

Galatians 4:6 *And because we are His sons God has sent the Spirit of His Son into our hearts, so now we can rightly speak of our God as Abba, our dear Father.*

Is that the secret of how the *Holy Nation* is established? We are the children of the Most High God and we can call Him Father. That my friends, makes us all related! We also have something else in common, that is the spirit of Jesus is in our hearts. See, there is not that much difference between us after all. We are God's family! My sisters and brothers and me!

Abba is an endearing way to address a father. There is much love and respect behind that connotation. Think how God would react to our prayers if we were to call Him *Abba.*

Why doesn't anyone on earth teach us that or better yet teach us and our children how to pray? Or teach the importance of prayer and the benefits of answered prayer? Remember it is about relationship, and prayer is the way to God. As examples of prayers, Luke 11 includes how Jesus taught His disciples to pray. John 17 has Jesus praying to His Father for His disciples.

A Prayer

Abba, I love and respect You, I render myself unto You. Teach me how to listen to You as well as talk to You. I realize that Jesus said in Mathew 18 that if two of us agree down here on earth concerning anything we ask for, my Father in heaven will do it for us. I then stand here with the reader of this prayer and ask of You to grant us knowledge, wisdom, understanding, and discernment of Your holy word. Amen

Week Seventeen

1st John 3:24 *Those who do what God says - they are living with God and He with them. We know this is true because the Holy Spirit He has given us tells us so.*

Obedience to the will of God is another brick in our building of a life. Not being obedient can be a major obstacle in not getting a prayer answered. It only makes sense. He created us, gave us guidelines to live our life with, and said He wanted a personal relationship with us.

It is impossible to be perfectly obedient, but that is no excuse for not trying! If we are being as obedient as we can, this verse says we are living with God. Wow! What else could you want but to be living with God?

John was the disciple who referred to himself as "the one whom Jesus loved". I believe John could not tell a lie, so if he said God gave us the Holy Spirit; then surely, we have the Holy Spirit with us. Halleluiah!

For those of you who practice reading around the verse, if I were you, I would look up all that refers to the Holy Spirit. Then I would let the Holy Spirit control every thought I had. How could you go wrong with that? Why isn't that being taught everywhere?

A Prayer

Jehovah Nissi, our LORD our banner, let Your spirit invade my conscientiousness and set me free. *Abba*, let all doubt pass before me and never to return. Amen

Week Eighteen

1st Corinthians 3:16 *Don't you realize that all of you together are the house of God, and that the Spirit of God lives among you in His house?*

It goes on to say that if anyone defiles and spoils God's home, God will destroy him. For God's home is holy and clean, and you are that home. The word "home" replaced the word "temple" in some Bible language. I think "temple" has more of an impact. Think of your body as a living temple. This is what we are in the process of constructing! Sounds pretty awesome, doesn't it? Why do some persons defile their own temple?

All of us make up God's house or temple. Do you see how holy God expects us to be? He sees us as priests in a holy nation, our bodies as temples. What would happen if we all worked together for the advancement of this holy nation? Do you think God would bless us endlessly?

The first step toward obtaining wisdom is to fear God. If you respect and fear God, you will hate evil. Wisdom hates pride, arrogance, corruption and deceit of every kind. Fear God and obey His commandments, for this is the entire duty of man. We are building wisdom bricks. Our foundation is as solid as it could be. For the last four months we have put together so many attributes of God, why would you not give up control of your life to His reign? He is the all-wise, all-good, all-knowing and loving God beyond measure, so why would you not join in His plan for man for your own sake if not for the love of God?

A Prayer

Jehovah Elohay, the LORD my God, thank You for Your Spirit, please let it take over for me. At this point, I see nothing else that makes more sense. Thank you. Amen

Week Nineteen

Psalms 111:10 *How can men be wise? The only way to begin is by reverence for God. For growth in wisdom comes from obeying His laws. Praise His name forever.*

Some language in other Bibles, use the word "fear" instead of "reverence"; "The fear of the LORD is the beginning of wisdom". I believe that while 'to fear God' does accurately portray a certain necessary element of our relationship with God, the focus here is He loves us! The Keeper of the stars is all-powerful and can do what ever He wants to do.

When King David wrote the Psalms the laws he was talking about were the Ten Commandments. Can you recite all ten of them?(Exodus 20) How can you obey if you do not know the laws? Do you realize that our country, America, was founded on these laws? In fact, you could not get a deed for a territory without signing a document stating that you would teach the Bible. Look at some of the early charters of early America and you will see that God blessed the United States of America for beginning their new country His way!

What must God be thinking when He sees groups like the A.C.L.U. stating there is a separation between state and church? That group is actually the Anti Christian Litigation Unit. We have got to start honoring God, or else face the wrath of God. Does 9/11 ring a bell?

A Prayer

Jehovah Elohim, the Eternal Creator, have mercy on America. We pray for our spiritual leaders to have strength and conviction to lead us back to your ruler ship. Father what would You have me to do? I am here for You. Amen

Week Twenty

Proverbs 7:4 *Love wisdom like a sweetheart; make her a beloved member of your family.*

King Solomon penned these words. He was reputed to be the wisest man that ever lived. Even if he wasn't, you would have to admit his way of telling us about wisdom was unique! God showered Solomon with abundant blessings so much that he was also one of the wealthiest men to ever have lived.

Let us see if we can describe how to treat a sweetheart but at the same time keeping in mind wisdom. *Respect* comes to mind first. *Honor* and *cherish* are a close second. Oh yea, how about *love unconditionally*? Of course never having enough of that special one, always wanting more, would be how to treat a sweetheart. Solomon said to treat wisdom that way.

What would you have to say to wisdom if you had a chance? Solomon said in The Living Bible, "Say unto wisdom, thou art my sister; and call understanding thy kinswoman. That they may keep thee from the strange woman, from the stranger which flattereth with her words". No beating around the bush here.

A Prayer

Jehovah Tsidkeenu, the LORD our righteousness, bless me with as much wisdom and understanding as You think I can handle. Open up Your Bible so that even I can see. I love You. Amen

Week Twenty-One

Proverbs 9:10 *For the reverence and fear of God are basic to all wisdom. Knowing God results in every other kind of understanding.*

"I, wisdom, will make the hours of your day more profitable and the years of your life more fruitful. Wisdom is its own reward, and if you scorn her, you hurt only yourself" was the next verse. Last week we wanted to ask questions of wisdom; this week wisdom answered.

How simple can it be? Knowing God results in EVERY other kind of understanding. The only way to know God is to keep reading the Bible, talking to Him reverently, and listening for His answers. Practice wisdom in what you do each day all daylong.

Because of this promise from God, let us cleanse ourselves from all filthiness of the flesh and spirit, doing what we want when we feel like doing it. The Holy Spirit will be convicting us trying to get us to perfect holiness in the reverence of God. That my friends is wisdom for all the ages! We have spent two months on wisdom. There is no excuse for not wanting as much wisdom as you can get. From a practical point of view why would you not want your days to be more profitable?

A Prayer

Abba, I humbly ask you to forgive all my confessed and unconfessed sins. I repent my former way of thinking, which wasn't very smart, and seek to learn as much as I can about You. Have mercy LORD. I praise your holy name. Amen

Week Twenty-Two-Foundation of Truth

John 8:32 *Jesus said unto them, "You are truly my disciples if you live as I tell you to, and you will know the truth, and the truth will set you free".*

Free as a bird flying across the bright blue sky. No worries, no pain, no sorrow, absolutely free! Freedom is the absence of restraint. We are finally getting somewhere. I didn't tell you that wisdom was worth two rows of bricks! It is time to push this along to the dizzying heights of our new life!

We are going to tackle the concept of truth. What is the truth? We are going to spend the rest of this book describing what the truth is. The opposite of truth is falsehood. Today many politicians and those who find the absolute truth inconvenient teaches that there is no truth, or whose truth you are talking about. To them it is all-relative. Hogwash! Who started that lie? Einstein himself said that one couldn't use relativity in a moral matter.

Friends, our kids are being taught that lie. Why is it that kids are killing kids? Why is it that babies are having babies? Abortion, that kills babies, has got to be stopped. Where there is blood, there is life. A fetus has blood. What are future generations going to say about we Christians who just sat by and did nothing? Will future generations look on us just as we look back at the Germans who were killing Jews by the thousands, while the world stood by and watched? The same can be said about slavery. Sometimes the truth convicts us to act. When Wisdom says for us to do something collectively, so we must. Wisdom and Truth are active concepts not passive!

A Prayer

Most gracious heavenly Father, let the truth be known. Father, lead us to that world where your truth prevails. May thy kingdom come and Thy will be done on Earth as it is done in Heaven. We pray that the truth be self-evident. Amen

Week Twenty-Three

2nd Timothy 1:7 *For the Holy Spirit, God's gift, does not want you to be afraid of people, but to be wise and strong, and to love them and enjoy being with them.*

Reading further in Verse 9, "it is He (Jesus) who saved us and chose us for His holy work, not because we deserved it but because that was His plan long before the world began, to show His love and kindness to us through Christ". That was Paul telling us about the plan of man by God on or around the sixth day of creation. For those readers who thought I made up the concept of God's plan for man, in Paul I am vindicated!

We are in search of the truth that can set us free. We know who God is, what He wants from us, and that God choose us long before the world began. Now that is a solid foundation! Do you think that God loves us? Let's make that assumption part of our foundation.

We are supposed to love people not fear them even though these people can be hard to work with. Only lack of knowledge in this case causes fear. Have you ever witnessed to anyone about your faith? Well, in the next three months, we are going to find irrefutable truth to bolster your faith. We are going to ask the Holy Spirit to open our minds and eyes and see how much God loves us. One of the greatest gifts he gave us is the talent to pray. Pray for others as well as for yourself.

A Prayer

How great You are LORD. Your mighty power that You shower all over us, strengthens us to the point where we do not fear people. With your love running through our bodies, I ask humbly to teach us the truth about your plan for man. Amen

Week Twenty-Four

Exodus 19:5 *Now if you will obey me and keep your part of my contract with you, you shall be my own little flock from among all the nations of the earth; for all the earth is mine.*

Verse 6 was discussed in Week 8. That is where you were to become a priest in a *Holy Nation*. There is that request by God again, "obey me". God does not ask much from us, yet so often we are not able or willing to do even the simple tasks that He asks.

The only way we are ever going to keep our part of that contract with God is to keep ourselves in the presence of God. No matter what kind of problem arises, there is nothing that God can't overcome. When we give up our self pride the "I can do this by myself" attitude in our lives, God promises us membership in His own little flock.

Maybe I should put in one paragraph here about Satan, because God sent him to rule His footstool the Earth. You can't deny Satan's existence because there has been a spiritual battle going on since recorded time. Satan's main game is to steal, kill, and destroy the love for God in the souls of men. He also puts doubt in peoples mind. He is that "fallen angel" that was previously mentioned. For a good explanation of why he was "kicked out" of Heaven, check out Isaiah 14: 12-17. That is enough said about that loser who will eventually be cast into Hell forever.

A Prayer

Father I ask that you teach me how to ward off the attacks by Your fallen angel. I realize he will come in many different disguises, even as light. You alone O' Holy One can protect me from the lies and doubts of the devil's fiery darts. Thank you God for your protection.
Amen

Week Twenty-Five

Psalms 99:7 *He spoke to them from the pillar of cloud and they followed His instructions.*

We have touched on the importance of prayer. This verse is just another example of God talking to man. Isn't that what prayer actually is? God isn't looking for brilliant men and women, nor is He depending upon eloquent men and women, nor is He determined to use only talented Christians in sending His Gospel out into the world.

God is looking for broken people at the end of their natural abilities. God's strength is for the weak, not for those who trust themselves too much. Beware in your prayer, above everything, of limiting God in any way. Think of what He can do, of how He delights to hear His children pray.

Satan hates it when you pray. So there is a very good tip on how to keep Satan out of your affairs. Let us come boldly to the Throne of Grace that we might obtain mercy and find help in our time of need.

We must find time to pray. Let all else go, but not your prayer time. Thank God for ten things before you get out of bed each morning. We have a lot to be thankful for. Most of all, don't forget to listen for God's voice!

A Prayer

Father, I thank You for the countless blessings You have bestowed on my life. Where would I be without You? Teach me LORD how to serve You better. Amen

Week Twenty-Six

Luke 11:28 *He replied, "Yes, but even more blessed are all who hear the Word of God and put it into practice".*

Jesus was telling a woman who was trying to bless the mother of Jesus for having Him; her action was ok to do. However, He made sure to distinguish "ok" from "blessed". Jesus certainly knew what was important to His Father in heaven and that was the focus was on Jesus and His ministry not His mother being part of that ministry

Another main point I saw to share were the words "hear the Word of God". First the word "hear", as in the verse from last week, while you are praying in peace and stillness, listen for God to speak. Another way to hear the Word of God is to pause while you read your Bible.

Knowing the Bible equips you to pray against the attacks from Satan. God assured us He would be there for us, but He wants to be sure you know how to best petition Him in your prayers.

Let's look at "putting it into practice". I believe there are at least two ways to do that. The first would be for you to live your life in the laws of God. Obedience, remember how important that was to God?

The second would be to witness to others. To tell the lost souls in the world about how great our God is. Pray on my friend!

A Prayer

Abba, You are great! Show me how to tell others about You. Please forgive me for my shortcomings. I yield my soul to You and Your way. Amen

Week Twenty-Seven

Ephesians 6:18 *Pray all the time. Ask God for anything in line with the Holy Spirit's wishes.*

Plead with Him, reminding Him of your needs, and keep praying earnestly for all Christians everywhere and that all souls may be led to Heaven. Other Bible language for this verse says, "And for me, that utterance may be given unto me, that I may open my mouth boldly to make known the mystery of the Gospel". The Holy Spirit charges us to go and tell others about the mystery of the Gospel. You will need God to do this.

Before you go out and witness for the LORD, you must put on the whole armor of God.(Ephesians 6:13-18) Here are some things you will need: 1) The strong belt of truth, 2) The breastplate of God's approval (righteousness), 3) Wear shoes that are able to speed you along as you preach the Good News of peace with God, 4) You will need faith in a never failing God as your shield to stop the fiery arrows aimed at you by Satan, 5) The helmet of salvation which is the totality of God's love, and 6) The sword of the Spirit which is the Word of God.

As witnesses for God, we will not be fighting against people made of flesh and blood, but against persons without bodies, the evil rulers of the unseen world, those mighty satanic beings and great evil princes of darkness who rule this world; and against huge numbers of wicked spirits in the spirit world. Your strength has to come from the LORD, because we do not even know what these spirits look like let alone how they fight.

A Prayer Arm me Father, and never forsake me I pray. I need You. Amen

Week Twenty-Eight- Prophecy

Psalms 16:10 *For You will not leave me among the dead; you will not allow Your beloved one to rot in the grave.*

Now we can begin to put the "cornerstone" in our new building of a life. Sometime in the 10th century BC, King David was telling us something that was going to happen in the future. He was explaining that there was going to be someone who died, but wouldn't be left in the grave. This must have seemed preposterous to those of David's time. Not even legend of that era could explain this phenomenon.

Prophecy is where we are going now. I want to show you over the next few weeks a few of the hundreds of prophecies that are contained in the Bible. The ones I have selected will talk about the coming of a Messiah. This Messiah would become the cornerstone of our new life and of the world. He was to be the Savior of the world. Realize right now, God spoke these words to David approximately 1,000 years before the birth of Jesus.

I could go all the way back to Moses' writings in the first five books in the Bible and show how God was making revelations to man about His plan for man. As I mentioned, there are hundreds of instances in the Bible that speak of Jesus before He was born, where He was to be born, and what would happen to Him, but we only want this book to be a one year long meditation!

A Prayer

LORD God I want to thank you for showing me the facts contained in Your inspired word. With quiet confidence I now go forward in opening my mind to see the truth. You are great and greatly to be praised!   Amen

Week Twenty-Nine

Isaiah 7:14 *All right then, the LORD himself will choose the sign-a child shall be born to a virgin! And she shall call Him Immanuel (meaning "God with us).*

200 years after King David lived, God called Isaiah, one of Israel's main prophets. Isaiah was just a man the same as you and I. There was only one difference; he had found favor with God because he had the courage to do what God asked of him. Isaiah had talked with God on numerous occasions, as is shown throughout the Book of Isaiah.

Again, I think that some people of that era must have been laughing at the concept of a virgin birth. In fact many today scoff at the idea of a virgin birth. Just because you can't understand how a virgin could get pregnant, doesn't mean it is not true! All Mary had to say to the scoffers of the truth and to save Jesus was to scream out, "Stop! I lied! I had my child by_________." You fill in the blank. She didn't, because she couldn't. It must have been true! How can we limit the power of God, who created man in the first place?

This is the first prophecy of a couple I selected because I want to show how hundreds of years before the event that was to be, was foretold by a priest of a holy nation. Sound familiar?

A Prayer

Abba, we see Your handiwork with Your prophets. We just thank you LORD for giving us Jesus the way You did. I realize that You talk to any man who has his heart with You. Blessed be the name of the LORD. Halleluiah! Amen

Week Thirty

Isaiah 9:6-8 *For unto us a child is born; unto us a Son is given; and the government shall be upon His shoulder. These will be His royal titles: "Wonderful", "Counselor", "The Mighty God", "The Everlasting Father", "The Prince of Peace". His ever-expanding, peaceful government will never end. He will rule with perfect fairness and justice from the throne of His father David. He will bring true justice and peace to all. This is going to happen because the LORD of heaven's armies has dedicated Himself to do it.*

You probably recognize these words from the Christmas pageants you have attended. 800 or so years before the birth of Jesus, in a time of uncertainty for the "chosen people", God spoke these words to the holy man named Isaiah. What don't the Jewish scholars understand about these words? It blows me away. With this verse plus the ones I'm going to lay out for you in the coming weeks, I just don't see how anyone can not see that Jesus was answered prophecy. The last perfect "correction" in God's plan for man.

It is my fervent prayer that God would open the eyes of mankind, and see there is no way other than what is written, that there was Divine intervention by God to "fix" the plan for man He started centuries ago.

In 800 years from this prophecy, God was going to release His chosen ones from the formalities of His laws and offer His grace instead. Our inheritance is freedom, absolute freedom in Christ!

A Prayer

Almighty and everlasting God, open the eyes of our Jewish brothers and sisters, and let the scriptures come alive to them. I know I have a plank in my eye, help me to remove it. LORD we pray for the peace of Jerusalem. Amen

Week Thirty-One

Daniel 7:14 *He was given the ruling power and glory over all the nations of the world, so that all people of every language must obey Him. His power is eternal – it will never end; His government shall never fall.*

We move 200 years ahead of Isaiah, and once again God bends down to communicate to man. Daniel had an interesting life. He went through captivity, was thrown in a lion's den, and later was promoted to a ranking position in a foreign government. Have you ever wondered why God foretold what was going to take place? Why didn't He just do it at that time?

What must Daniel and Isaiah and the other prophets been thinking about the dreams they were having? Do you think maybe God is granting dreams today of any magnitude?

Through prophecy God let it be known exactly what His plan for man was going to be. There was going to be a leader who will rule the world forever. Jesus is the only one that can fulfill that prediction. He came, He saw, He conquered. He is coming again, but we will get to His prophecies later.

A Prayer

Our Father in heaven, hallowed be thy name. We glorify You and your gift of grace. Thank you for choosing us to be with You forever. What a humbling thought! Amen

Week Thirty-Two

Micah 5:2 *O Bethlehem Ephrathah, you are but a small Judean village, yet you will be the birthplace of my King who is alive from everlasting ages past.*

Micah lived somewhere between 739 – 693 BC, which would put him near the time of Daniel. Now the question of all questions in this book: "What don't our Jewish scholars see about this prophecy?" Who else was born in Bethlehem that would rule as King from ages past to eternity? Please get back to me on that one. I would love to hear you make a fool of yourself. To deny the divinity of Christ in one's lifetime may look foolish on Judgment Day before the Throne of Christ.

Humble your pride my Jewish friends, and see the truth. I invite you to ponder my last question. I know this sounds unbelievable to you. Jesus is the answer to the question, and you and I crucified Him 2000 years ago. Please forgive us Father for we knew not what we did.

As you can tell, the message of this writing is getting stronger. I give all glory to Jesus and the Holy Spirit who fill these pages with words of truth. 2nd Timothy 3:16 says God inspired the writing of the Bible, and Isaiah tells us in 40:8 that God promised to preserve the Bible through the centuries. The Bible is the only book for me!

A Prayer

Jehovah Elohay, the LORD my God, all glory and honor to You. We praise your holy name. Your plan of man, which included Jesus, is bigger and more grandiose than anything man has ever accomplished. Open the eyes of all your creation to see Jesus. We thank you and thank you and thank you! Amen

Week Thirty-Three

Zechariah 9:9 *Rejoice greatly, O my people! Shout with joy! For look – your King is coming! He is the Righteous One, the victor! Yet he is lowly, riding on a donkey's colt!*

What? A donkey's colt for my King? Absolutely, God's ways are different from those of man. The Jews of this era expected a Messiah to lead them to peace. Horses were for war! No wonder they missed this prophesy in Zechariah when Jesus rode a donkey's colt into Jerusalem that first Palm Sunday! He was the King of all Kings, the Prince of Peace.

God knew how proud and stubborn men can be, especially the way the chosen ones had been. Do you think you would have understood that event on the first Palm Sunday if you happened to be there to see it? I believe it is very necessary to seek wisdom in all matters concerning Scripture lest you might miss something important for lack of wisdom.

If you want to see where your knowledge is at, read Revelation and try to interpret it using events in today's world. What is going to happen in the Middle East? A lot more of the plan for man is also laid out in other parts of Revelation, Ezekiel, and Daniel to mention a few. We just might be the generation that sees Jesus coming again for His Church!

A Prayer

Most gracious heavenly Father, lead me to wisdom in the matters of the future. Open my eyes and help me to discern the events so described in Scripture. Amen

Week Thirty-Four

Zechariah 12:10 *Then I will pour out the spirit of grace and prayer on all the people of Jerusalem, and they will look on Him they pierced, and mourn for Him as for an only son, and grieve bitterly for Him as for an oldest child who died.*

Brothers and sisters, I ask you now, do you understand what I meant by a plan by God for man? This prophecy was spoken almost six hundred years before Jesus was crucified. Some cynics say Jewish historians of biblical times wrote these prophecies in after the fact. Hogwash! Good try Satan!

Zechariah was classified by Jewish scholars as one of the Minor Prophets and as such would be mentioned in the Torah, the teaching part of Judaism. Next week's verse is from another one of these Minor Prophets who also had important work to do for God. Your life may seem minor also yet you are important to God just the same. I ask my Jewish scholarly friends, "What criteria did you use for coming up with classifying prophets?"

I know I am asking questions, but I am hoping you are too. There can be no doubt about who Jesus is, why He came, and what happened to Him while He was walking on the Earth. I hope we are well on our way to removing all doubt! You are worth it!

A Prayer

Jehovah Shammah, the LORD is present, I come unto you in praise with much joy. Thank you O' Holy One for granting us Your grace and heavenly mercy. *Abba*, there is none like You! Praise You Almighty One, all honor and glory to You! Amen

Week Thirty-Five

Malachi 3:1 *Listen: I will send my messenger before me to prepare the way. And then the One you are looking for will come suddenly to His Temple-the Messenger of God's promises, to bring you great joy. Yes, He is surely coming, says the LORD of Hosts.*

Now who in the world could Malachi be talking about? I said that with tongue-in-cheek! Of course it is John the Baptist, who even said he was brought forth to prepare the way of Jesus!

Each prophet wrote about who and how the Messiah would come but none of these writers had the total concept of what God was going to do. If they did know, why didn't they write it down? They just wrote down what God told them to do. Malachi is the last writer in the Old Testament. He was living around the time of Zechariah, a little over five hundred years before Jesus was born.

What if Christopher Columbus had prophesied that one day we could fly over the Atlantic in a fraction of time spent in his day? This is what I am talking about. Daniel 9:24 almost called the very day Jesus would be born! God had to have spoken to these writers because there is no way they could have had this knowledge. I marvel in how they fit together and how incredible these prophecies were, and that it is only possible because God planned it that way. Jesus fulfilled each and every one of them. That is beyond probability! The Cornerstone of our building a life in the family of man is now complete!

A Prayer

Thank you God for showing me how wonderful your plan for man is! I know You love us as Your very own. Teach me how to love my enemies.   Amen

Week Thirty-Six

Malachi 4:6 *His preaching will bring fathers and children together again, to be of one mind and heart, for they will know that if they do not repent, I will come and utterly destroy their land.*

Ok, let me see, place of birth, when born, what His purpose was, how He would be treated, how he would die, and what effect He would have on mankind, all written several hundred years before Jesus was even born. I am amazed that some just can't see it!

Webster's dictionary defines *repent* as "to feel such regret over an action or intention as to change one's mind". That was John the Baptist's message to all who would listen. We hear a voice in the wilderness, calling God's creation to repent of their sins. That means you too Israel! It is our habits and attitudes which we take for granted that makes us so hurtful to God.

This wraps up the prophecy part of this book. Next we will ponder who this man named Jesus was; and see if He is the Son of God. Maybe before we move on, we should take this time to repent of all of our confessed and unconfessed sins, and ask that the blood of Jesus make you clean!

A Prayer

Father, I humbly ask You to forgive me all of my confessed and unconfessed sins. I want to be a new creation in Christ. Gather me under Your protective wings. Amen

Week Thirty-Seven- Jesus

Mathew 1:1-17 *These are the ancestors of Jesus, a descendant of King David and Abraham…*

The proof of Jesus' family tree line is there for all to see. The names throughout that bloodline reads like a "Who's Who" of God's greatest men! Jesus came from a royal Hebrew line. Read the Book of Luke 3:23-38, and see how far that line really goes back. That is how He claims the title of 'King of kings'.

We may not be part of that royal line by birth, but we can be joined into that line through the acceptance of the instructions Jesus gave us as our King. Hey now, we have come full circle in the 'Holy Nation of Priests'. I was getting a little impatient waiting to get to Jesus in this book, so now that we are here, let's crown Him the 'King of our Holy Nation' and find out how He fulfilled prophecy.

The next three weeks we will do just that. Our foundation is getting so strong that it could bear any number of bricks of facts to our building, and handle it with ease!

A Prayer

Jehovah Elohay, the LORD my God, I thank You for Jesus and how He made Your plan of man so wonderful. I accept Jesus as my King and Savior and offer my heart to You O God. Fill me with Your Holy Spirit and set me free from my sins.   Amen

Week Thirty-Eight

Mathew 2:1 *Jesus was born in the town of Bethlehem, in Judea, during the reign of King Herod.*

To refresh our memory, Week 32 gave us Micah's prediction of this event, which was written over seven hundred years before it happened! Micah gave the exact place where it was to happen! So much for thinking this one of Israel's prophets was 'minor' to God!

More amazing is Daniel's prophecy (9:24-27), in which his "seventy weeks" counts out almost to the day Jesus was born. That glorious day, on which Angels sang in the sky, and most importantly time was split in half! There was one epoch before Jesus and there was another after He was born. Halleluiah, Amen!

Just think, the very first Christmas morning. The first gifts were given by shepherds and then came the Magi bearing gifts. Jesus was God's gift to man. Have you "unwrapped" Him yet?

I was just checking as to where your thoughts are. The whole purpose of this book was to remove all doubt about Jesus' claim to be the Son of God as part of God's plan for man. When He was born in the manger, the prophecies of Weeks 29-36 came true. These were just a few of the ones listed throughout the Old Testament. What is the probability of one man justifying every one of them?

A Prayer

Jesus, I welcome You to come into my life to be my Savior and King. I am sorry for trying to run my life, please forgive me. Abba, I thank You for the gift of Salvation through the birth of Jesus that first Christmas morning. Praise Your Holy Name. Amen

Week Thirty-Nine

John 1:1 *In the beginning was the Word, and the Word was with God, and the Word was God.*

Here the "Word" referred to is none other than Jesus. Read the rest of that chapter when you have time. Before anything was created God the Father existed, there was Jesus, in and of God. He has always been alive and is Himself God. He created everything there is – nothing exists that He did not make. Eternal life is in Him, and this life gives light to all mankind. His life is the light that shines through the darkness, and the darkness can never extinguish it. The Holy Spirit will lead you to understanding the divinity of Jesus through sincere prayer.

I have quoted the words of my Bible to show you the meaning of verses 1-5. I have read other versions where Verse One says "and the Word became flesh". Ponder that for a moment. I suggested earlier in this book that I can't wait to sit at the feet of Jesus, and ask for some explanations of "Heavenly things".

I ask for discernment now, but it comes so slowly. So I have to accept God's word as fact, and that will have to do! Maybe before the end of this book God will reveal some of those answers I seek. Reason is the aid and servant of faith, yet faith can still stand where my reason and comprehension do not reach.

A Prayer

Almighty and Everlasting God, to You all honor and glory. Thank You for Jesus our King, Savior, Counselor, Morning Star, the Lamb of God, and the Lion of Judah. If it be Your will, please reveal Your secrets to Your chosen ones. Thanks be unto You. Amen

Week Forty

John 1:6 *God sent John the Baptist as a witness to the fact that Jesus Christ is the true light.*

John himself was not the true light; he was only a witness to identify it. According to John 1:29, John the Baptist pointed Jesus out to the people telling the crowds, "This is the One I was talking about when I said, Someone is coming who is greater by far than I am, because He existed long before I did". Malachi in Week 35 prophesied about John the Baptist as a messenger from God. Malachi, Haggai, and Zechariah were the last prophets and prophecy in the Old Testament came to end with their deaths, that is, until Jesus began His ministry.

The Jewish leaders sent priests and assistant priests from Jerusalem to ask John the Baptist whether he claimed to be the Messiah. John denied it flatly and said he was not the Christ. They wanted to know who he was, to be speaking with such authority. He replied, "I am a voice from the barren wilderness, shouting as Isaiah prophesied to get ready for the coming of the LORD".(John 1:19)

Further in the Gospel of John Chapter 1, John the Baptist told them "He baptizes with water,... but right here in this crowd is someone you have never met who will soon begin a ministry among you, and I am not even fit to be His slave. Look! There is the Lamb of God who takes away the sins of the world. He is the One I was talking about". If you were there would you have recognized Jesus?

A Prayer

I see Him! There He is! LORD Jesus here I am! Amen

Week Forty-One

Colossians 1:22 *In the body of His flesh through death, to present you holy and unblameable and unreprovable in His sight.*

In other words, Jesus has done this through His death on the cross of His own human body, and now as a result Christ brought you into the very presence of God, and you are standing there before Him with NOTHING left against you. There is NOTHING left against you, with NOTHING left that He could even chide you for. What else could a sinner like us ask for?

We got to Week 41 by all the prayers that we prayed together. God has promised to forgive every sin you ever did. Believe it because this is true. Jesus is the One we owe everything to.

It is all in God's plan for man, which included this remarkable event in time. Do you understand that through Jesus you are spotless in God's eyes? You, that priest in a holy nation, your slate of sins are wiped clean. Are you jumping up and down with this news?

The rest of this book will be all about Jesus. We will be adding brick upon brick atop our foundation of a new life. Mathew 10: 38 tells us that Jesus Christ asked us to follow Him with our crosses. What must we do to satisfy Him? Stay tuned!

A Prayer

Jehovah Mekaddiskem, the LORD our sanctifier, thank You for the free gift of grace through Your son Jesus. I lift mine eyes unto You LORD, and pray in all thanksgiving for forgiving me my sins. How happy You have made me! Blessed be Your Name forever! I want to live my life for You, show me what to do. Amen

Week Forty-Two

1ST John 1:9 *If we confess our sins, He is faithful and just to forgive us our sins, and to cleanse us from all unrighteousness.*

This confession of sins requires each of us to be introspective and undo our bad habits. "Going through the motions" with no intention to improve offends God even more than the sin we confess. Verse Ten says, "If we say that we have not sinned, we make Him to be a liar, and His word is not in us". God is not a liar. So we now can say that every man is a sinner, no one excluded.

As previously mentioned in this book, all God wanted was for us is to be righteous. Jesus makes us righteous in God's eyes. Without Jesus, God cannot even see you in His presence. Praise upon praise for Jesus, our King, everything to Him I will bring!

If we are righteous, and we are in God's presence, what would we expect to happen? What you should be asking is why would I expect anything? Just to be in God's presence is awesome, so I suggest that you bask in His glory and get lost in His love. He is the great provider, the Great I Am, and has promised us an abundant life in Christ. Are you with me? A righteous priest under the Kingship of Jesus Christ, in His Holy Nation, is what we aspire to be.

A Prayer

Father, in Jesus' name I ask you to show me how to get an abundant life in Your Holy Nation. In Jesus' name, I pray, that I can believe I am "spotless" in Your eyes. Amen

Week Forty-Three

Job 22:18 *Yet He filled their houses with good things: but the counsel of the wicked is far from Me.*

To truly understand what this verse means, you should probably read the whole book of Job. We have prayed for discernment and this is an example of my suggestion earlier in this book to read around the selected verse for understanding why God put this in the Bible.

The people of Job's time were saying to God, "Go away, God! What can You do for us?" You have got to be kidding me! All the miracles in Egypt were still in their collective minds. It seems all that man does is whine and whine and whine.

God forbid that I should say a thing like that! I look around me and only with my renewed life in Christ do I see God's hand in everything. It does not matter where I am, or who I am with, God is as alive today as He was in Job's time. Some scholars say that Job was the first book written.

People could not understand then or even now, the idea of a sovereign God. I plead for you to quit quarreling with God. Agree with Him and you will have His promised peace at last! His favor will surround you if you will only admit that you are often wrong. Listen to His instructions and store them in your heart, and then do the good He asked!

A Prayer

Father, I thank You for never giving up on me. I confess how rebellious I really was. I give You all honor and glory for my life. Spotless in Your eyes, I humbly ask for more wisdom to make me whole. In Jesus' name I ask you to grant me discernment as well. Amen

Week Forty-Four

Psalm 105:24 *And He increased His people greatly and made them stronger than their enemies.*

This begs the question why? Why does God choose certain persons when He decides to move? God has said He would always choose the Jews and from within their ranks a God appointed prophet would come forth with instructions for all to follow.

These prophets followed God's instructions and relayed them to the priests of their time. Do you think that these prophets prayed much? How many blessings from God would come our way if we were all being obedient to Him. Do you think that a prayer of theirs might include, "The commander of the heavenly armies is here among us! He, the God of Jacob, has come to rescue us." I believe those prophets reminded the people how God always did miraculous things for them at their time of distress.

Come everyone and clap for joy! Shout triumphant praises to the Lord! For He alone is the God above all gods and is too sacred for words. He is the great King of the Earth! Being filled with the Word of God builds strength. This is the attitude to have so as to be stronger than your enemies. Then God will increase you beyond you wildest dreams!

A Prayer

Father I waited patiently for You to help me. I listened for Your voice and I know You heard my cry. You lifted me out of despair and set my feet on a hard, firm path and steadied me as I walked along. Thank You for a new song to sing. LORD, I trust in You alone. In Jesus' name I pray, Amen

Week Forty-Five

Acts 4:24 *And when they heard that, they lifted up their voice to God with one accord, and said, LORD thou art God, which has made heaven and earth and the sea and all that in them is.*

How many times have you included words like these in your prayers? This verse was part of a prayer the people were praying for the miraculous release from jail of Peter and John. Did you read around this verse? So, then you would know the reason they were being held by the authorities? Were the 'prayers' successful in getting God to move?

Sir Isaac Newton (1642-1727) in one of his dissertations said, "I can take my telescope and look millions of miles into space; but I can go away into my room, and in prayer, get nearer to God and heaven than I can when assisted by all the telescopes in the world". One-on-one prayer with God in a private setting is what Newton is referring to.

Ole Hallesby (1879-1902) in his book *Prayer,* said prayer was something deeper than words. It is present in the soul before it has been formulated in words. He went on to say it abides in the soul after the last words of prayer have passed over our lips.

We must be in one accord with God today. Won't you pray with me to ask God to intervene in the affairs of man? Let's lift up our voices and let the world know how great our God is!

A Prayer

Abba, You are our creator and we give thanks to Your power and glory. Hear our prayer LORD; rescue us from the threat of our liberties being taken away in America. Amen

Week Forty-Six

Psalms 91:16 *With long life will I satisfy him and show him my salvation.*

This long satisfying life and salvation is the "reward" for a soul who did something right: virtue, good habits, repentance and reparation. This quote wraps up the baptism, confession, communion discussions in past Weeks. It would be very appropriate at this time to say, and it is good to say, "thank you" to the LORD, to sing praises to the God who is above all gods. What a promise of our wonderful LORD!

Do you see how much His plan for man was to exalt man above every living thing? He gave man 10 commandments to follow and some did but most couldn't do it. Look through Leviticus and see how many rules God gave to His people. It is my opinion that God did this just to show how corrupt we are. I think He knew that it was going to take something "more" to save mankind.

That "more" was Jesus. John 3:16 says that God loved the world so much that He gave His only son so that *ANYONE* who believes in Him shall not perish but have eternal life. God didn't send His son into the world to condemn it, but to save it! Jesus is the salvation that the writer of Psalms was talking about.

A Prayer

Father, the reader and I humbly come to you in Jesus' name, and ask for Your mercy. We throw ourselves at Your feet and ask for Your help. Fill us with Your Holy Spirit and bless us LORD like only You know how. Thank You, Father. Amen

Week Forty-Seven

2nd Peter 3:18 *But grow in grace and in the knowledge of our LORD and Savior Jesus Christ. To Him be glory both now and forever. Amen*

Did Jesus create the plan for man? That would be another question for us while at His feet. All I know that if it wasn't for Jesus and what He did for us, I just don't know where or what I would be doing, what about you? I just can't see how people can be happy without Jesus.

Growing in grace and knowledge is a process over the years of a life well lived. Notice that the plan God has for man is broad and general as in the coming of a prophet, a battle or new dynasty; but God's plan includes an individual plan for each of us. This plan within a plan was in God's mind when He thought of creating you.

In Week 2, as you remember, Jesus said He was the "Alpha and Omega" (A and the Z), the first and last. We spent months talking about wisdom; in Week 22 Jesus said you would know the truth and the truth shall set you free! Are you any wiser now that you have read this book, meditated, prayed and improved your habits? I hope so!

Actually, it isn't this book that gives you wisdom; it is the Bible and what use you make of it. All I have done was to try to inspire you to think. The big decision to turn to God is only the biggest decision you will ever make. Get ready for the wise cracks and stares from unbelievers. Pray for them!

A Prayer

Almighty and everlasting God, we praise Your holy name. Blessed be the God of Israel. Father we want to serve You, have patience LORD, as we are almost ready for battle. Pour out Your spirit upon us and present us holy and unblameable. In Jesus' name, Amen

Week Forty-Eight

2nd Thessalonians 2:13 *But we must forever give thanks to God for you, our brothers loved by the LORD, because God chose from the very first to give you salvation, cleansing you by the work of the Holy Spirit and by your trusting in the Truth.*

Now there is the truth. 48 weeks and we finally got there. God knew you before you were even born! He knew you would be reading this book. In fact He knew I would be pounding my brain writing this book. I told you once I take no glory for this work. Every time I sit down to write more, I am amazed what is on the page.

We must continually give thanks to God for His plan for man. He created a "family of man". Because of His love for His family, He taught us how we can love others as well. Now there is some truth to discern.

The Holy Spirit is our friend. Micah 3:8 says we are full of the power of the Holy Spirit. It should be your very best friend. There will be times you will want to pray and words just don't seem to work. Turn it over to the Holy Spirit and God will hear your prayer. Never doubt that your prayer is heard by God. That is not cool. Luke 11: 8-9, says persistence will open the door, so keep on asking!

A Prayer

Most gracious heavenly Father, we love You and we praise Your holy name. How can we ever thank You enough for Your plan of man? You created us and have led us to the Truth, who is Jesus. In His name we pray and ask for forgiveness of our sins. Amen

Week Forty-Nine

John 14:6 *Jesus told him, "I am the Way - yes, and the Truth and the Life. No one can get to the Father except by means of me".*

Jesus was answering Thomas who showed how much he didn't understand about Jesus. Did you see in the next verse Jesus said to His disciples that they have seen God? Wow! I wonder what you are thinking about what Jesus said to Thomas.

Please allow me to ask, who else in known history of man ever made the claim of being the "Way, Truth, and Life"? Mohammed didn't, Buddha didn't, Confucius didn't, and neither have the founders of other major religions. Knowing all the recorded miracles, signs and wonders attributed to Jesus when He walked on the earth, how could anyone deny His claim that no one can get to the Father but through Him?

Friends, the picture is getting very clear. Our new life building, complete with a Cornerstone and a solid foundation, is still in need of completion. We are in the last month of our journey to a new birth of ideas and we just need to add a few "extras" to the building!

A Prayer

Father, when I think of what it is that You have done for us, words become inadequate. It is times like this that I can only smile, take a deep breath, and bask in Your love. The only thing I can say is thank you from the bottom of my heart. In Jesus' name I pray. Amen

Week Fifty

Hebrews 10:7 *Then I said, "See, I have come to do your will, to lay down my life, just as the Scriptures said I would".*

Jesus was the last known prophet in the New Testament; that is to say, He told exactly what was going to happen to Him before it did. He came in to the world because the blood of bulls and goats never satisfied God, it being a precursor and enlightenment to His people. That is why His body was made ready to be laid as a sacrifice upon God's altar, to be slain on a cross for each of us. He came to give His life for you and for me. Do you see God's plan in this? Didn't Jesus just confirm all the prophecies?

Jesus consummated the first system used by the Jews of sheep and calves for centuries yet supplanted it with this new plan having been forgiven and made clean by Christ's dying for us ONCE and for ALL. The old system of priests offering bloody sacrifices could no longer take away the sins of man. With the sacrifice of Jesus, God the Father said He wouldn't remember our sins and lawless deeds any more.

Since sin has been forever forgiven and forgotten, there is no need to offer more sacrifices to get rid of them. Now we have a fresh, new, life-giving way which Christ has opened up for us by tearing the curtain, His human body, to let us into Heaven and into the holy presence of God. Hallelujah, amen.

A Prayer

Help my faith Father; grant me the confident assurance that something I want is going to happen. Make it a certainty that what I hope for is waiting for me, even though I can't see it up ahead. Praise Your Holy Name!   Amen

Week Fifty-One

Revelation 19:10 *Then I fell down at his feet to worship him, but he said, "No don't! For I am a servant of God just as you are, and as your brother Christians are, who testify of their faith in Jesus. The purpose of all prophecy and all I have shown you is to tell about Jesus".*

John, who was in exile at this time, was telling us what the Angel of the LORD was telling him on the Island of Patmos. Jesus was the spirit of prophecy. The purpose of ALL prophecy was Jesus and what would happen to Him. Jesus said to the Pharisees that He would rebuild "the temple" in three days. Of course hc was referring to His temple, His sacred the body! He said he would rise from the dead in three days. Thus we have the story of Easter morning.

Realize that Christmas is the beginning of the Easter story. Christmas alone will not suffice. Easter sets Christianity high above every other man made religion by claiming resurrection from the dead by its Leader. Mohammed, Buddha, and Confucius are still in their graves, waiting for judgment day.

Did you notice that the Angel of the Lord said to John that we are just like him? We are all servants unto God in His Holy Nation! Congratulations, you made it. The only thing left is the last prophecy.

A Prayer

We thank you Jesus for giving your life to take away our sin. We humbly offer ourselves as a sacrifice to You. Please accept it has our gift to You. In Your name, Amen.

Week Fifty-Two

Revelation 22"20 "*He who has said all these things declares: Yes, I am coming soon! Amen! Come LORD Jesus!"*

It has been a little over two-thousand years since Jesus spoke these words to John, so let us wait patiently and confidently in hope that it won't be much longer. We all ask, come LORD Jesus.

Well, here we are a year later, and still waiting for Jesus to return. Let us use our time well! There is much I left out on how to live your life. All I wanted to do was to demonstrate how God the Father created a plan for man on the sixth day of creation. That plan was *The Family of Man*.

God is our Heavenly Father and His name is Holy. All believers have prayed for over 2,000 years that His Kingdom come and that His Will be done, and that Heaven and Earth be united in doing His Will. Many have asked God to take care of their daily needs.

We will be judged at death. Jesus will judge us as we have treated and judged Him and our fellow man in our respective lifetime. So we must forgive all who sin against us so that we may allow Jesus to pardon us all our sins. Then and only then will He keep us from all evil. As you might have noticed, God's plan for man was in the Lord's Prayer. May God bless you abundantly!

A Prayer

LORD God almighty, bless the readers and their loved ones. Grant them Your protection from all harm. Shower them with Your love. Bolster their faith in You, and bless them with courage to pass on the Gospel of our Savior Jesus. In Jesus name I pray, Amen.

www.ingramcontent.com/pod-product-compliance
Ingram Content Group UK Ltd.
Pitfield, Milton Keynes, MK11 3LW, UK
UKHW061830190726
13855UKWH00005B/1737